*"Nature is not
a place to visit.
It is home."*

—Gary Snyder

D1518585

For Vivi

FOREST

Christie Matheson

PA PRESS

PRINCETON ARCHITECTURAL PRESS · NEW YORK

The forest is…

filled with trees

and their
trunks and
branches,

needles
and leaves.

It has trills and tweets,

food to eat,

holes to
explore,

and tunnels
galore.

It has webs that glisten

and owls who listen,

nooks for nesting

and beds for resting.

It's a fun play space

and a hiding place.

It's
shelter
from
a storm.

The forest is...

home.

Taking Care of Our Forests

Forests are beautiful to see from far away and magical to
explore when you step inside. They are also very, very important
to our planet! Forests are full of trees, which help to keep the
air clean and the earth cooler and healthier.

Forests make you healthier too. Spending time in a forest
is good for your mind and your body!

And forests provide homes for millions of different plants
and animals—from tiny bugs to birds and butterflies to big bears—
all around the world. If forests are cut down, lots of those
animals lose their homes.

We can all do our part to help keep our forests healthy.
When you visit a forest, make sure you don't disturb any animals'
homes or leave any trash behind. Because paper is made from trees,
you can help save forests by recycling paper and asking your family
to choose products (like toilet paper!) that are recycled, tree-free, or
forest-friendly. And encourage your family to help organizations that
plant trees by volunteering or supporting them in other ways.

Or plant a little tree in your own backyard!

If you and your family want to learn more about
helping forests, visit:
The Nature Conservancy: nature.org
National Forest Foundation: nationalforests.org
One Tree Planted: onetreeplanted.org
Arbor Day Foundation: arborday.org

Published by
Princeton Architectural Press
A division of Chronicle Books LLC
70 West 36th Street
New York, New York 10018
papress.com

© 2024 Christie Matheson
All rights reserved.

Printed and bound in China
27 26 25 24 4 3 2 1 First edition
ISBN 978-1-7972-2849-5

No part of this book may be used or reproduced in
any manner without written permission from the publisher,
except in the context of reviews.

Every reasonable attempt has been made to identify
owners of copyright. Errors or omissions will be
corrected in subsequent editions.

Editor: Kristen M. Hewitt
Typesetting: PA Press

Library of Congress Control Number: 2023029338